FAMOUS LIVES

The Story of
ANNIE SULLIVAN
Helen Keller's Teacher

FAMOUS LIVES
titles in Large-Print Editions:

The Story of Louisa May Alcott: Determined Writer

The Story of Muhammad Ali:
  Heavyweight Champion of the World

The Story of Roberto Clemente: All-Star Hero

The Story of Bill Clinton and Al Gore: Our Nation's Leaders

The Story of Hillary Rodham Clinton:
  First Lady of the United States

The Story of Walt Disney: Maker of Magical Worlds

The Story of Frederick Douglass: Voice of Freedom

The Story of Benjamin Franklin: Amazing American

The Story of Jim Henson: Creator of the Muppets

The Story of Martin Luther King, Jr.: Marching to Freedom

The Story of Abraham Lincoln: President for the People

The Story of Thurgood Marshall: Justice for All

The Story of Pocahontas: Indian Princess

The Story of Colin Powell and Benjamin O. Davis, Jr.:
  Two American Generals

The Story of Jackie Robinson: Bravest Man in Baseball

The Story of Sacajawea: Guide to Lewis and Clark

The Story of Junípero Serra: Brave Adventurer

The Story of Sitting Bull: Great Sioux Chief

The Story of Annie Sullivan: Helen Keller's Teacher

The Story of Squanto: First Friend to the Pilgrims

The Story of Harriet Tubman:
  Conductor of the Underground Railroad

The Story of George Washington: Quiet Hero

The Story of Laura Ingalls Wilder: Pioneer Girl

The Story of Malcolm X: Civil Rights Leader

FAMOUS LIVES

The Story of
ANNIE SULLIVAN
Helen Keller's Teacher

By Bernice Selden
Illustrated by Eileen McKeating

Gareth Stevens Publishing
MILWAUKEE

J
B
Sullivan

For a free color catalog describing Gareth Stevens Publishing's list of high-quality books and multimedia programs, call 1-800-542-2595 (USA) or 1-800-461-9120 (Canada). Gareth Stevens Publishing's Fax: (414) 225-0377.

Library of Congress Cataloging-in-Publication Data

Selden, Bernice.
    The story of Annie Sullivan: Helen Keller's teacher / by Bernice Selden ; illustrated by Eileen McKeating.
        p. cm. — (Famous lives)
    Includes index.
    Summary: A biography of the woman who taught a deaf-blind girl how to communicate with others.
    ISBN 0-8368-1467-3 (lib. bdg.)
    1. Sullivan, Annie, 1866-1936—Juvenile literature. 2. Teachers of the blind-deaf—United States—Biography—Juvenile literature. 3. Keller, Helen, 1880-1968—Juvenile literature. [1. Sullivan, Annie, 1866-1936. 2. Teachers. 3. Women—Biography. 4. Keller, Helen, 1880-1968. 5. Physically handicapped.] I. McKeating, Eileen, ill. II. Title. III. Series: Famous lives (Milwaukee, Wis.).
HV1624.S84S45   1997
371.91'1'092—dc20
[B]   96-30700

The events described in this book are true. They have been carefully researched and excerpted from authentic biographies, writings, and commentaries. No part of this biography has been fictionalized. To learn more about Annie Sullivan and Helen Keller, refer to the list of books and videos at the back of this book or ask your librarian to recommend other fine books and videos.

This edition first published in 1997 by
Gareth Stevens Publishing
1555 North RiverCenter Drive, Suite 201
Milwaukee, Wisconsin 53212 USA

Original © 1987 by Parachute Press, Inc., as a Yearling Biography. Published by arrangement with Bantam Doubleday Dell Books for Young Readers, a division of Bantam Doubleday Dell Publishing Group, Inc. Additional end matter © 1997 by Gareth Stevens, Inc.

The trademark Yearling® is registered in the U.S. Patent and Trademark Office. The trademark Dell® is registered in the U.S. Patent and Trademark Office.

Printed in the United States of America

2 3 4 5 6 7 8 9 01 00 99

For my wonderful father, Julius Selden,
who like Annie turned his life around

With thanks to the Writer's Room
in New York City, where the book was written

Contents

FAMOUS LIVES

The Story of
ANNIE SULLIVAN
Helen Keller's Teacher

Housewife, Age Eight

S HE WOULD BE SO PRETTY, IF IT WERE NOT for her eyes!" That's what a neighbor of the Sullivans said, bending down for a closer look.

Eight-year-old Annie had a lovely round face, a fine turned-up nose, and lots of thick dark hair. But those soft blue eyes were clouded over. She did not see too well. And much of the time there were things she did not want to see.

Annie was a very unhappy little girl.

She had no idea that one day many would go out of their way to hear her speak. She would meet interesting and famous peo-

11

ple—inventors, writers, even presidents. She would travel in several countries and be written about in newspapers and magazines. Her life would be devoted to a great service.

As it was, Annie knew only that she was among the poorest of the poor. Her parents had fled the Great Famine in Ireland during the "hungry forties" (the 1840s), as that time was called. They came to the United States.

Thomas Sullivan, Annie's father, worked on a farm in a tiny town in Massachusetts called Feeding Hills. Like so many unskilled laborers, he made very little money.

But being poor was not the major cause of Annie's unhappiness. She was very sad because her mother had just died. And of the five children born to that gentle ailing woman, it fell to Annie, the oldest, to keep house for her father. Since the other children were living with relatives, there was just Annie and Thomas, who was, more often than not, drunk and insulting.

Sometimes Annie did naughty things and didn't know why she did them. Once, when her father was shaving, she threw something at the mirror he was using. It fell to the floor in pieces. "You little devil!" he said, shaking her violently. "Look what you brought to this house. Bad luck for seven years!" There were times that Annie wondered if she really was the cause of all the family's troubles.

But there was a soft side to Thomas Sullivan. He enjoyed telling her stories. One story was about the Little People who had followed him, he said, straight from Ireland. They had magical powers and could do both good and evil. When Annie asked him where the Little People lived, he told her that they were under a large flat rock in front of their house. How many times Annie tried to lift that rock! But it was much too heavy and she could never find the wee elves.

And Mr. Sullivan was very concerned about Annie's eye problem. One day he took her to nearby Westfield to have her eyes examined by a doctor. So that she would feel good about the visit, Mr. Sullivan bought Annie one of the most beautiful hats in the world. It was white with a large brim and a ribbon the color of her eyes, set off by a velvety red rose.

Then came the unsettling news. "Your

13

daughter has trachoma," the doctor told Mr. Sullivan. "Her eyes are inflamed and will always be that way." Apparently, Annie had contracted the eye disease three years earlier when a younger sister lay dying of a terrible fever.

Mr. Sullivan sighed. "Ah, if we were only back in the ould counthry, in dear old Limerick. The River Shannon is there and its waters are holy, *holy*, I tell ye! They were tears from the eyes of the Lord—tears of joy when he beheld my Ireland with its beautiful green lands. Why, a single drop of it would cure the lass, I am sure of that."

A man who drank away his small earnings and a girl who could not see too well were not able to keep house for long.

Living in Feeding Hills, among other Sullivan relatives, were Thomas's brother John and his wife, Anastatia (called Statia— "STAY-shuh"—for short). John grew tobacco on his farm and was able to buy a large house for his family.

Although Annie's parents had had five children, there were only three alive at this time—Annie, the oldest, Jimmie, now five, and Mary, just out of babyhood. While Annie was keeping house for her father, John and Statia were taking care of the smaller children. Now they had to take Annie as well, which they did with mixed feelings. Annie was not known to be an easy child to handle, and because of her eyes she was unable to go to school.

She spent most of her time playing in the big red tobacco barns and wandering the hillside. She tended John's cows as they grazed on the "feeding" hills, but often would just let them wander off into a neighbor's field.

At Christmastime, Annie heard that there would be presents for everyone, including herself. She watched the unwrapped gifts pile up in the front room and fell in love with a wonderful doll that had long blond hair. Annie was sure that the doll was for her. She would always remember that Christmas morning and the shock of seeing the doll handed over to one of Statia's daughters, while she received a toy that seemed less than worthless.

Thomas Sullivan had promised to provide for his three children, but John and Statia never received a penny from him. They lost patience. They had children and expenses of their own and could not handle the load of caring for relatives. So little Mary was sent to live with another aunt, while Annie and five-year-old Jimmie were simply told they would be going on a long trip.

Jimmie had been born with a disease called tuberculosis, the one his mother had died of. It affected his hip, which had a round lump on it, and he walked with a crutch. Jimmie had never been away from Feeding Hills. Where were they being sent? Annie wondered. No one would say.

On Washington's birthday, February 22, a wagon came rolling up to the house. Relatives had begun to gather around, but still nothing was said about where the children were going. They knew only that at Springfield they would be taking a ride on a railroad train.

Statia tried to kiss Annie before she mounted the wagon. Annie pushed her aunt away.

"You might at least be a good girl on the last day," Statia said.

The last day? Then they were being sent away for good!

They went to Springfield and took a train to Boston where they were met by a man who told them very little as he took them to another station. It was a cold day and Annie held Jimmie close, to quiet his shivering. They became part of a surging crowd, more people than they had seen in a lifetime, and finally took their places in a high-ceilinged railroad coach.

Annie had the feeling she would never return to Feeding Hills. And that turned out to be correct. Her family now was just Jimmie.

Alone in the Poorhouse

THE TRAIN LET THEM OFF AT TEWKSBURY, a town not far from Boston. A long dark windowless carriage awaited them. This carriage was called a "Black Maria" and it was usually used to take tough criminals to prison. The two weary children were hoisted inside by the tall man, who then quickly departed.

Again, they were not told that their destination was the state's poorhouse, or "almshouse" (*alms* means money given in charity to the poor).

In the hallway of the poorhouse someone came to take their names and finally told

19

them where they were. Next to the names it was noted that ten-year-old Annie was "virtually blind" (although she could see more than anyone knew) and that tiny Jimmie was lame, with a tubercular lump on his side.

A gray-haired man, who looked official, gave the order: "The girl must go to the women's ward, and the boy to the men's."

Annie set up a wail that brought heads to doorways to see what was the matter. Because his sister was crying, Jimmie began to cry, too. "We want . . . to be . . . together," he said, nearly choking on his tears.

The man glanced from one to the other. "You may be together," he said understandingly, "but James will have to wear an apron, just as the girls do."

The children were too relieved to be shocked. The first night they slept in a room by themselves with a bed, a table, and a small altar of the kind used in churches. Later they were told that this was the "dead house," where bodies were taken to be buried. The next day they were given beds side by side in the women's ward.

Annie would not let her frail brother out of her sight. They cut pictures out of magazines and pasted them all over the walls of the "dead house." Annie's eyesight was so poor she sometimes cut off the heads of her paper dolls. Because of this she turned over the fine work to Jimmie. With leftover pages, Jimmie cut out long strips and used them to tease the rats and mice out of their corners, making them run crazily around the rooms. This amused Jimmie, but frightened the inmates.

But more and more Jimmie was in pain. He grew so ill that the doctor finally warned Annie that soon her brother would be going on a journey. Annie was wild with worry, for she did not want to lose the one human being she truly loved.

After only a few months in the poorhouse, little Jimmie died and was laid out in the very "dead house" where they had played. Never before or afterward did Annie feel so lost and alone.

The poorhouse at Tewksbury was not like our institutions today. The healthy and the sick lived together. There were also thieves

and drunkards and poor people who didn't have jobs.

Sometimes as the women watched the procession of men who went before them to the dining room each day, one would cry out: "There go the Horribles!"

Sometimes a lone voice would lift up in song. It was usually an Irish ballad and, one by one, all would join in. One was called "Rocked in the Cradle of the Deep." Annie did not know that "deep" meant ocean, and if she had, she would have been little the wiser, for she had never seen an ocean!

She liked to pretend. Once a blind woman asked her what she looked like. Instead of describing herself, she described the Christmas doll at Anastatia's house.

"I am very beautiful," Annie said. "I have blond curly hair down to my waistline, jet black eyes, and long, long lashes."

But one of the girls described what Annie really looked like. "Oh, Holy Mother of God, child!" the woman said. "Why can't you tell a poor blind soul the truth?"

Maggie Carroll, an older woman, became a good friend. Her body was so twisted by a wasting disease that she had to be strapped into a chair in order to sit up. She read many books aloud to Annie. The books had to be placed on a rack that had been especially set up for her. Maggie's nature was so lovable that people adored her and couldn't do enough for her. Annie, who was put in charge of distributing medicines each day, always saved the best painkillers for Maggie.

Every week a Catholic priest would visit the Tewksbury poorhouse. One Sunday a new priest arrived. His name was Father Barbara. He took a liking to Annie and would pat her on the head with his large gentle hand. "This is no place for you, little woman," he would say. "I'm going to take you away from here, I promise."

Father Barbara did take her away. Exactly one year from the time she had arrived, he took her to a charity hospital in Lowell, Massachusetts. There she had her first eye operation. The operation relieved her of the little colored flecks that had danced in her eyes, but her vision remained poor.

Annie loved the nuns who were her nurses, with their neat white bonnets and their smiles. She stayed at the hospital for several weeks, going for walks with Father Barbara along the Merrimack River. She visited poor families with the Sisters, carrying baskets of fruit and cakes. She was allowed to make her own lemonade by breaking chips off the big ice block in the hospital's icebox.

Finally they said she could go home. But where was "home"? The church had called Father Barbara to another part of the country. With great disappointment, Annie was sent back to Tewksbury.

Conditions there were getting worse, if that was possible. The state of Massachusetts spent $1.75 a week for each person in the poorhouse. Additional buildings were needed to house the ill and the insane. The superintendent begged for a barn in which to keep cows. If he had cows, he said, he could feed the milk to the babies, who were now dying soon after birth.

In 1880, four years after Annie first arrived, she heard that there was to be an investigation of Tewksbury. The man being sent by the State Board of Charities was Frank B. Sanborn. Annie decided that when he came, she would try to get his attention. Perhaps, like Father Barbara, he could help her to leave. But this time she wanted it to be for good and always. Some of the inmates had told her about schools where blind people were taught to read and write. In fact, they said, there was one only twenty miles away.

Annie followed the men making the tour, preparing the speech she would tell the one who was Mr. Sanborn. "There he is!" someone said, just as the group was about to leave through the yellow gates of the poorhouse.

"Where? Show me!" she said breathlessly. The man pointed to a tall man walking ahead of the others.

Annie ran up to Mr. Sanborn, nearly knocking him over.

"Mr. Sanborn—I want to go to school. Please, please listen to me."

"What is the matter?" he asked in a kindly and interested voice.

"I . . . I can't see very well."

"Oh? And how long have you been here?"

Annie paused. She was ashamed because she had not counted the years.

"A very long time," she said sadly.

"I will try to get you into a school," Mr. Sanborn said. "I have one in mind. You just wait a while."

Much to her joy, the "while" turned out to be only one week. She got word that she would be admitted to the school she had heard about—the Perkins Institution for the Blind. It was unbelievable luck.

Just Like
the President's Wife

ANNIE WAS CATAPULTED FROM JOY TO misery on her very first day at the Perkins Institution. Although she was fourteen years old, she was put into a sewing class with nine-year-olds. The class was speechless when she said she had never held a needle.

"How old are you?" the teacher asked.

"I don't know," she said.

"Where do you come from?"

Annie was not about to announce to the world that she came from a miserable almshouse. "I don't know," she answered again, blushing.

In another class she was unable to spell

some simple words, words everyone else knew. The class laughed at and ridiculed her.

She was the only girl who had arrived at Perkins without a nightgown, a comb, a hat, a coat, or a pair of gloves. Someone had to lend her a nightgown on her first night. It was a night she spent mostly weeping, missing the rough and ready friends she had left behind in Tewksbury.

Perkins was located in Boston, for years one of the most important cities in the United States. It was a place where philosophers, writers, and artists gathered to talk about world affairs. Someone described it as "the City of Kind Hearts."

Among the kind hearts was Samuel Gridley Howe, the founder of the Perkins Institution for the Blind. Back in the 1830s, many years before the Civil War, Howe had spoken out about the evils of black slavery. Later his wife, Julia Ward Howe, would write a song about the antislavery struggle, *the* song of the Civil War, "The Battle Hymn of the Republic."

In 1832 Howe had just returned to Boston from Greece, where he had helped that country fight off the oppression of the Turks. A friend, riding with Howe through the streets of Boston, told him about a plan for a school for the blind. Would he help to get it started and then run it? the friend wanted to know.

From that day, work with the blind became Howe's great cause.

For centuries blind people had been considered to be of little worth to society. Some were beggars, storytellers, buffoons. Some roamed the countryside in groups, living from hand to mouth. Others stayed at home their entire lives, secluded and separate from the rest of the world.

Howe was determined to help blind people receive the kind of education and training that would help them to become "active" citizens. He set up the Perkins Institution for the Blind. Soon he became world famous, particularly for his work with Laura Bridgman. Laura was a deaf and blind child Howe encountered on a trip to New Hampshire. He brought her back with him to Perkins and worked with her patiently until she was able to recognize words and to communicate, in a simple way, with others. Laura would live out her days at Perkins, a living testament to his care and genius.

In 1880, when Annie arrived at the institution, Howe was no longer living. His place had been taken by a dynamic man he had met and brought over from Greece, Michael Anagnos.

Annie was still a difficult person to handle. She had tantrums and talked back to teachers. Once, when the mathematics teacher asked her, "When is your brain awake?" she shot back—"When I leave your class!"

Anagnos grew increasingly fond of Annie, but she tested him to the extreme. One time she lied to him, saying she was going to the Eye and Ear Infirmary in Boston. Instead of going there, she attended the hearings at the State House about conditions in Tewksbury. When Anagnos learned about this, he was furious and almost expelled Annie. Later he forgave her, but began to call her "Miss Spitfire."

In time Annie's bitterness about life softened. Loving teachers took her in hand. But best of all there was Mrs. Hopkins.

Mrs. Hopkins was the new housemother in the cottage where Annie stayed. She had lost her daughter, an only child, and decided to devote her life to the blind children at Perkins. She and Annie informally adopted each other, and Annie spent heavenly summers and vacations at the older woman's home in Brewster, on Cape Cod.

Annie soon began to realize that she, herself, was not only very smart, but also attractive.

When she was about sixteen, Anagnos sent her on a mission that showed his confidence in her. She and another young woman were asked to visit newspaper publishers in Boston. They were to ask them to advertise Perkins' need for money. Anagnos wanted to build a kindergarten for blind children.

The dark-haired, blue-eyed teenager charmed the editors. One of them told her he would publish the notice if she paid him. Annie had not been given any money to spend.

"Oh, we can't pay," she protested.

The editor smiled and said, "I think you can, young lady. With a kiss."

"Oh my, yes," Annie said, pleased. It seemed like a small enough price to pay. She pecked the man on the cheek and skipped out.

By this time Annie had had five eye operations, but it was the next two that made a difference. For it was these operations that took her out of the category of "virtually blind." And the way it happened was almost accidental.

During her second summer at Perkins, Annie took a job doing light housekeeping in a boardinghouse in Boston. One of the men living there, who had been reading aloud to Annie, took an interest in her vision problems. There was, he said, a brilliant doctor in the city who had a great gift for eye surgery.

Annie was taken to the Massachusetts Eye and Ear Infirmary, where the doctor performed one operation, then after a year, another one. When Annie's eyes were healed, she was overjoyed. *She could read!* No greater gift in life could have been given to her.

Since most of the residents at Perkins were blind, the lighting was dim. Often Annie had to lean way out a window with her book to catch the last bit of sunshine for the day. She read all the poems, novels, and magazines she could put her hands on.

By the time she graduated Perkins, in 1886, Annie was head of her class of eight students. She was twenty years old. At the ceremony it would be Annie who delivered the honored valedictory speech.

Mrs. Hopkins, her beloved housemother, designed her graduation dress and provided a pink sash that her daughter had worn for her high school graduation. Mr. Anagnos had said once that Annie looked like President Grover Cleveland's wife. Mrs. Hopkins fixed Annie's hair to look like Mrs. Cleveland's, piling it on top of her head, with little ringlets on her forehead.

Annie stood before the audience of twelve hundred people who had turned out to see the graduation. On the platform the governor of Massachusetts called out her name. Annie sat frozen for a moment. When the governor spoke her name again, she rose,

34

trembling. The speech was well received. Annie spoke about how important it was for every person to educate himself, in spite of the hardships of life, and gave thanks for the "abundant opportunities" that had been given to her.

Afterward Annie removed the white dress and with a towel carefully brushed off her shoes, the first white ones she had ever worn. She tearfully fingered the tiny pearl buttons of the dress, then packed it up in tissue paper, wondering what she would now do with her life.

The poorhouse at Tewksbury stood in her mind as a trap she might fall back into. What would she do if she were forced to return there and grow old with Maggie and all the pained and twisted women she remembered, the pitiful rejects of the world?

She decided she would worry about the future later and enjoy her moment of glory. She put the corsage that had been pinned to her belt in a glass of water and went to the dining hall with her head held high. "No one will know," she said to herself, "that I'm not the happiest girl in the world. . . ."

Before the Miracle

I N 1880, IN THE STATE OF ALABAMA, FAR AWAY from Massachusetts, a baby girl was born. The family was far different from the one Annie was born into. The baby's father, while not rich, earned enough as an editor, and later as a federal marshal, to keep the family quite comfortable.

The mother was considerably younger than her husband and was charming and vigorous. She raised two stepsons. This baby was the first of her own three children.

When the child was about eighteen months old, a fever of unknown origin swept through her little body. Her parents were very happy when the fever finally went away. Many sick children living in that time never recovered.

But in a short while both parents noticed that something was wrong. Their daughter did not blink when objects or people were close to her. She did not smile or reach out or repeat words like *mama* or *papa,* as she had done before her illness.

The little girl was deaf and blind. Touch, smell, and taste were the only senses she could use to learn and know about the world.

The name of this girl was Helen Keller.

By the time she was six, Helen had developed into a very pretty child and one with a lot of energy and spirit. She needed all the energy and spirit she had, because much of what was going on was lost to her.

But even though Helen had no words to use at all, she still managed to show, in a limited way, what she had on her mind.

If she wanted ice cream, she made signs with her hands imitating the turning of the handle of the ice-cream machine. If she wanted her father's attention, she mimicked the way he read the newspaper. She developed several signals for her mother.

She could help fold laundry and knew her own clothing from others'. She played with the children whose parents were employed on the property. She knew insects and recognized pets by feel.

But there were feelings Helen could not express. She was in a world she did not understand. Often the things she thought she needed, she could not get. So she had temper tantrums all the time and did impish and damaging things. Objects had a way of slipping away from her, of getting turned over, of being smashed.

And she lashed out—by pinching her grandmother, by locking her mother in the pantry, by overturning her baby sister's cradle. Some of her relatives called her a "wild, destructive little animal."

Captain Keller (called "Captain" because he had fought in the Civil War) was in despair. He wrote to Alexander Graham Bell, who was then living in Washington. Only ten years earlier Bell had become famous as the inventor of the telephone. Because he had a deaf wife and was a kindly and compassionate man, Bell took an interest in Helen. He was to be her friend for the remainder of his life.

Through Bell, Captain Keller eventually reached Michael Anagnos. Could Mr. Anagnos find a companion and teacher, he asked, for his blind and deaf daughter? There was ample space in his home, and, for the moment, Keller felt he could pay as much as twenty-five dollars a month.

Anagnos thought Annie was the right person for the job. He sent a note to her at Cape Cod where she was spending the summer with Mrs. Hopkins. Annie was excited at the idea of working with Helen. But before taking on the task, she wanted to return to Perkins, for there were things she needed to find out to prepare for her work.

Anagnos wrote to assure Captain Keller that Annie would "make an excellent instructress and most reliable guide for your little daughter."

It was now fifty years since Samuel Gridley Howe had brought Laura Bridgman, the deaf-blind child, to Perkins. The world had largely forgotten his accomplishments, and Laura herself was a quiet religious middle-aged woman who kept to herself and busied herself with needlework.

After teaching Laura to read with raised letters, Howe adapted the manual alphabet (the sign language of deaf people) to communicate with her. Annie had learned this alphabet while still a student at Perkins, and was able to tap out short conversations against the palm of Laura's hand.

Now she studied Howe's records to see how he and some of the other teachers had worked on this project. And she was beginning to develop her own ideas about what she might do.

By March 1887, Annie was ready to make the trip to Tuscumbia, Alabama, where the Kellers lived. Mrs. Hopkins gave her a "good dress" to take along, making over one of hers designed with pretty purple flowers. The rest of what Annie took was the simple sturdy kind of clothing made more suitable for New England living than the mild climate of the South. She also took a doll bought for Helen by the girls at Perkins.

41

Laura Bridgman had sewn a little outfit for it.

With little experience in long-distance travel, Annie with the "help" of Mrs. Hopkins bought the wrong kind of ticket from the agent. Annie was obliged to change trains many times, and to make one lonely sleep-over stop. The cinders and coal dust stirred up by the railroad train irritated her sensitive eyes. Then, as she proceeded farther south, she saw that the wardrobe she had brought was totally wrong—her gray woolen dress was beginning to feel like a fur coat! She arrived in Tuscumbia three days after she had started out, perspiring and tired.

Each day before her arrival, someone from the Keller family had gone to meet the trains at the station. Just when they were beginning to wonder if their new employee was ever going to come, Annie descended from the train. James Keller, Helen's stepbrother, walked up to her and smartly shook her hand. He seemed cold and perhaps amused. But Mrs. Keller was a surprise to Annie. She was just a few years older than Annie and

spoke most pleasantly. When Mrs. Keller smiled, Annie's entire day brightened.

James drove a wagon in a slow leisurely way to Ivy Green, where the Kellers lived. The one-mile trip along tree-lined dirt roads seemed to last forever. Later Annie realized that *all* of life slowed down in the South.

Captain Keller was waiting on the lawn. He looked imposing in a formal suit, with dangling watch chains. He, too, shook her hand. "So happy you could come," he said.

"Where is Helen?" Annie asked, shivering with excitement, warm as she was. She had had so many pictures in her mind of the seven-year-old girl, and couldn't wait to see what she was really like.

They Fight

As they came closer to the house, Annie saw a child half-hidden in the doorway. She was well formed and had a beautiful face. But her apron was soiled, her hair uncombed, and the white laces on her black shoes were mostly untied.

"There she is," Captain Keller said. "She has known all day that someone was expected, and she has been wild ever since her mother went to the train station to get you."

"How could she have known someone was expected?" Annie asked.

"Oh, she knows a great deal," Mrs. Keller offered. "She can feel the vibrations of people, and also of animals, about the house."

Meanwhile, Helen lunged at Annie, nearly knocking her backward against Captain Keller. She put her hands to Annie's face, then touched her dress and the small traveling bag she was carrying. She pulled at the catch to see if the bag would open.

"She wants to know if you have any candy there," Mrs. Keller said. "Sometimes our guests bring little gifts. Here, let me take it."

"Just wait . . ." Annie pulled out a watch to distract Helen, who was beginning to get flushed and make angry sounds because she could not have the bag.

Annie showed her how to release the cover of the watch by putting her fingers on the spring. She did this several times. She also managed to "tell" Helen, by placing her hand on the trunk, that there *was* a treat in store for her later, if she would be patient.

In Annie's room Helen helped her put her things away. She groped for and found Annie's hat as soon as she had removed it, and put it on her own head. It was amusing to see her primp in front of the mirror, just as if she could actually see herself in it. No doubt she was imitating someone she had felt going through those motions.

Then Helen reached into the trunk and pulled out the gift doll from the blind girls at Perkins.

Annie decided to start her lessons right then. Curling her fingers against the palm of Helen's hand, she spelled out D–O–L–L in the manual alphabet she had learned with Laura Bridgman.

She pulled the doll gently away from Helen, intending to return it when she got Helen to spell D–O–L–L herself. Helen's face again got red, and she grabbed the doll from Annie's hand. She was used to getting her way. For a few seconds there was a tug-of-war as Annie tried to get hold of the doll.

"You don't understand . . ." Annie began, before she realized this child could not hear. She tried to get Helen into a chair so that she could start the lesson over again, but gave up, exhausted. She had to try something else.

Down in the Keller's big kitchen she saw a large cake, only half eaten. She cut a piece, wrapped it in a cloth napkin, and brought it upstairs where she found Helen sulking.

Into Helen's hand she spelled C-A-K-E, allowing her to unwrap the sweet bundle only after Helen had made the same motions in Annie's hand. Helen ate the cake very quickly, afraid it would be taken away from her.

The next morning Annie came down to a peaceful family scene in the Keller's dining room. While Captain Keller ate his breakfast slowly and thoughtfully, Mrs. Keller was chatting with her stepsons, James and Simpson. James was just a little younger than Annie, and Simpson looked about age twelve or thirteen. In a corner of the room, in a cradle, baby Mildred lay sleeping.

Suddenly Helen came thundering into the room behind Annie. Annie took her seat, but Helen remained standing and sniffing the aromas of the food. To Annie's horror, Helen began going from place to place, taking a bit of food from each person's plate and stuffing it into her mouth. To her even greater shock, not one person in the family did anything about it, much less make some remark.

When Helen tried to take a piece of bread

from Annie's plate, Annie moved her plate out of reach.

Helen then pinched Annie.

Annie slapped Helen.

Helen lay down on the floor, kicking and grunting and trying to pull Annie's chair out from under her. She was determined to have her way.

Confused and disturbed about these goings-on, the family one by one tiptoed out.

Helen returned to her chair and started to eat—but with her hands instead of a spoon. Annie insistently placed a spoon in her hand. When the meal was over, Helen threw her napkin on the floor. They struggled until, at Annie's insistence, Helen folded it. Finally Annie let her run out and play while she went up to her room and had herself a good cry.

"I suppose I shall have many such battles with the little woman," Annie wrote Mrs. Hopkins, "before she learns two essential things—obedience and love." But she wished in her heart it could be otherwise.

At the Water Pump

THIS WAS A DIFFICULT TIME FOR ANNIE. Often she wondered if she could find the jewel of a child buried under the resistant wild creature.

Helen's movements were so angry that once her hand flew up and knocked out one of Annie's front teeth.

"To get her to do the simplest thing, such as combing her hair or washing her hands," Annie reported to Mrs. Hopkins, "it is necessary to use force." But then the family would get upset, particularly Captain Keller, who could not bear to see his daughter cry.

Something had to be done—Annie thought—and quickly.

Was there a place she and Helen could be by themselves? she asked the Kellers. Surprised by this request, they promised to think it over.

Finally Captain Keller made available to them a garden house some distance away from Ivy Green. "But only for two weeks," he said firmly. "Then we want her back home."

Day by day Helen became easier to work with. But it was an up and down struggle. One morning, during the first week in the garden house, Captain Keller passed by and looked in the window. He saw Helen still in her nightgown long after the breakfast hours. He was outraged. "I've got a good mind to send that Yankee girl back to Boston," he told a relative.

He had no idea what progress this "Yankee girl" was making. Helen was learning to sew, knit, and string beads. On her daily visits to the barnyard, she was beginning to identify living creatures.

"I spell into her hand everything we do all

day long, although she has no idea yet what the spelling means," Annie wrote.

The two weeks in the garden house passed quickly, and soon teacher and student were back in the Keller home.

Helen was beginning to associate some of the words with some objects out there in the world. It was a kind of game that she played, partly to please Annie. But she was mixed up about a lot of things.

For instance, she knew that the words *mug* and *milk* had something to do with drinking. But she kept using one in place of the other. Now, when she was washing her hands, she asked to know the word for *water*. She did this by pointing to the water and patting her teacher's hand.

Annie took her out to the pumphouse in the garden. Helen felt the cold water pouring into her mug and all over her fingers. Annie spelled W–A–T–E–R into her free hand. Helen froze. She looked as if she was remembering something from very long ago. As Annie reported it: "The word coming so close upon the sensation of cold water rushing over her hand seemed to startle her. She

dropped the mug . . . A new light came into her face."

Helen had suddenly realized that she was not just playing games, but that *words* stood for *things*. And if she could identify those things with words, she had the power to know anything she wanted to—out there in the world of light and sound.

She touched the ground and immediately wanted to know the word for it. Then the pump. When her baby sister was brought out for her to hold, she wanted to know what she was called. And finally she wanted to know Annie's name.

"T–E–A–C–H–E–R," Annie spelled out. From that day on, Annie was called "Teacher" and nothing else.

A key had been turned in Helen's mind. Within an hour she had memorized thirty words.

"When I got into bed," Annie wrote, "she stole into my arms of her own accord and kissed me for the first time, and I thought my heart would burst, so full was it of joy!"

"Helen is a truly wonderful child," Annie wrote to the director of Perkins a few weeks later. "She knows almost three hundred words and is learning five or six a day."

Anagnos wrote back: "I am deeply interested in your pupil. She certainly is a remarkable child. Keep an exact account of what she learns and does every day." And he began to keep records also, putting Annie's accounts of Helen's progress into his annual reports, reports that were widely read.

Whatever interested Helen in the wide world, her teacher would explain in detail. "Everything that could hum, or buzz, or sing, or bloom" was part of her education.

Helen became conscious of her appearance. She liked to wear pretty dresses and to have her hair put up in curls. She learned to count and to read simple books written in the raised letters of the alphabet. She seemed to want to know everything.

Then came the day she asked to be able to write letters to people. Teacher got her a specially designed board for blind people, grooved so that a pencil could form letters on the paper placed over it.

This is Helen's first letter, written to her

mother, when Helen and her father were away on a trip.

> Helen will write mother letter
> papa did give helen medicine . . .
> conductor did punch ticket papa
> did give helen drink of water . . .
> helen will hug and kiss mother.
> good-by.

The following letter was written to her mother just one year later, and shows how rapidly Helen got command of the written language:

> My dear Mother, I think you will be
> very glad to know all about my visit
> to West Newton. Teacher and I had a
> very lovely time with many kind friends
> . . . I was delighted to see my dear little
> friends and I hugged and kissed them . . .
> Clifton did not kiss me because he does
> not like to kiss girls. He is shy . . .
> Will you please ask my father to come
> to the train to meet Teacher and me?
> . . . With much love and a thousand kisses
> from your dear little daughter.

In the year between the two letters, the "wild animal" had become a brilliant and joyful child. Already she was expressing herself better than Laura Bridgman.

At Christmastime, Mrs. Keller told Annie, "I thank God every day in my life for sending you to us." Captain Keller took her hand, but could not speak. His heart was too full of emotion.

The following year in the Perkins Institution's report, Anagnos included the full story of Helen's awakening. Later he took that section and had it printed as a separate pamphlet. He included photographs of Helen's letters and commented, "This tiny author is a most extraordinary individual." He called Annie Sullivan "the miracle worker."

Alexander Graham Bell published one of Helen's letters to him in a New York newspaper, and her fame began to grow. The Keller family was upset, however, when a newspaper reporter turned up on their doorstep late at night. They did not let him come in.

When they visited relatives in Memphis,

Tennessee, Annie and Helen discovered they were celebrities. It seemed that half the city's population came to see them. Annie wrote to a friend, "Helen was petted enough to spoil an angel, but I do not think it is possible to spoil her. She is too loving."

From the time she awoke each day to the time she went to sleep, Helen picked up information about her world. Then when she learned to read braille, the raised-dot system of the blind, a whole universe of knowledge was opened to her.

Annie would no sooner explain something when questions would fly from Helen's fingers: *Why?* . . . *How many?* . . . *Who?* . . . *When?* . . . *Where?* She even learned phrases in foreign languages and included them in her letters.

There came a time when Annie felt that all she had to offer, all that could be done for Helen in Alabama, was not enough. What would be the next step in Helen's education?

The Price of Fame

MR. ANAGNOS HAD BEEN FOLLOWING Helen's progress closely. He knew that sooner or later Helen would need still more education. And he had a sense that the world was waiting to see this famous child.

He wrote to Captain Keller. Would he consider having his daughter and her teacher visit Perkins Institution for a few months? Helen could then make use of their facilities and equipment, and she would have a chance to be with other blind children.

The Kellers discussed the idea. They wanted very much to keep Helen at home, and Annie with her. But they suspected that it was time for the two to move on. Captain Keller finally said *yes,* and Mrs. Keller got busy making Helen a wardrobe of pretty clothing.

Helen was now famous enough so that the President of the United States wanted to see her! So, on the way from Tuscumbia to Boston, they stopped off in Washington, where President Cleveland received them "in a very large and beautiful white house" with "lovely flowers and many trees and broad smooth paths to walk on"—as Helen described it, relying on her teacher's observations, as always.

Annie was disappointed that Mrs. Cleveland did not appear. She wanted to see if she really looked like her, as Mr. Anagnos had said.

At Perkins, Helen was delighted to find children and adults who could "talk" in the manual language. With the other pupils she learned beadwork and clay modeling and how to read maps and use typewriters.

Annie was receiving more compliments from teachers, teachers of seeing children

as well as deaf and blind children. Everyone wanted to hear her story.

In addition to spending time at Perkins, Annie and Helen visited writers they admired. One was the poet Oliver Wendell Holmes. Teacher, as always, described everything she saw and heard to Helen and acted as interpreter for Helen's words. After they had been in Dr. Holmes's sitting room for a time, Annie was astonished to see the black woman who worked there burst into tears. "That child is so wonderful," the woman said. "I have a sister who is blind and she just wastes away in an asylum."

But when people get famous, there are always some who doubt them and sling mud at their reputations.

There were times when Helen was treated like a star, while Annie was ignored. Or worse, Annie might be treated as a kind of servant girl who just happened to be around when Helen decided to become a genius.

Then there were some who thought that Helen was nothing—a puppet of Annie's, a mere empty shell waiting to be filled.

These people no doubt felt justified when a piece of Helen's called "The Frost King" was published. Helen was only eleven at the time, but everything she did was noted by the press and public. When it was discovered that a very similar story had been published years earlier, Helen and Annie were on the carpet. It was a very trying time for them both. Helen was criticized and called a hoax, just for repeating a few half-remembered phrases in a story. It was truly unfair.

At the age of sixteen Helen decided that she wanted to go to college. She applied to Radcliffe College, which just a few years earlier had been created for women as an "annex" to Harvard University.

The college dean was against having her there. How could she possibly go to school with normal girls if she could neither see nor hear? How would she manage the class exams? Even with Annie at her side, could she keep up with the professors' lectures?

Helen and Annie went ahead with boning up for the exams, which consisted of such subjects as English, German, French, and

Greek and Roman history. Annie was not permitted in the room when Helen took tests. Helen read them in braille and typed the answers. When the results were in, they were delighted to find that Helen had passed all her subjects "with credit in Advanced Latin."

Annie was used to being Helen's eyes and ears, but the amount of work that loomed ahead in the next four years would be a tremendous strain for her. Books that were not printed in braille (and most of the textbooks were not) would have to be read and spelled into Helen's hand. Foreign words would have to be looked up in dictionaries.

And Annie had to perform the almost impossible feat of listening carefully to the professors and at the same time spelling into Helen's hand what they were saying.

Some people said, "Why don't they just say that Miss Sullivan is entering Radcliffe, instead of Helen Keller, a blind, deaf, and dumb girl?"

The worst of it was that Annie was getting warnings from doctors that if she did not have another eye operation soon, her vision would get worse.

There was no time or money for the operation, and Annie continued to read for Helen, trying to rest her eyes whenever she could.

A Book Is Born

THEY HAD BEEN AT RADCLIFFE COLLEGE
two years when a visitor showed up at the
door of one of the classes. He wanted to see
Helen Keller, he said. Annie and Helen
came out into the hallway. Would Helen be
interested in writing five articles for the
magazine *Ladies' Home Journal*? he asked.

Helen looked puzzled. How did he know
she could write those articles? And how
could she and Annie both work on something so extensive, when it was all they could
do to keep up with the flow of college work?

"Tell him I couldn't possibly do it. Not
now," she spelled into Annie's hand.

"Do take it," Annie spelled back. "He is paying three thousand dollars. Do you know what that will mean for us? And besides, it's about time people knew the *true* story of your life."

Helen had been writing themes for one of her English classes. Her teacher was Charles T. Copeland, known affectionately by his students as "Copey." He encouraged her to write about her own experiences, even when she insisted that no one could possibly be interested. *He* would be interested, he said. Before too long Helen had become the best writer in the freshman English classes. Annie and Helen guessed that it was Copey who had tipped off the *Ladies' Home Journal* that there was this treasure in the heart of Radcliffe.

After they wrote their first article, the women ran aground. It was turning out to be more work than they had expected. When was the second article coming? the *Journal* editors kept asking.

Just at this time one of their friends introduced them to John Macy. Macy was a brilliant professor of English literature, just starting out in his career. He was also an editor of *Youth's Companion,* a magazine that Helen had written for. He might be just the person to help them with their writing.

Macy turned out to be an editor, agent, and friend rolled into one. He was a tall and handsome man, in his twenties like Helen, with a shock of thick dark hair.

Finally Annie could take something of a rest while John picked up the reins. He learned the manual alphabet and was able to work closely with Helen.

When the five articles were completed, it became apparent that they could easily be made into a book.

It was John who sold the book idea to Doubleday and Company, and on March 21, 1903, the first day of spring, *The Story of My Life* appeared. A few months later Helen would be twenty-three years old.

Annie had more to do with the book than she had expected to. After Helen had told her story, with many letters written by her included in the text, there was still one question unanswered.

How did the "miracle" occur? What ex-

actly had happened that liberated the seven-year-old "animal" and made her an intelligent and joyful human being? If there was a secret, the secret lay in those early months when Annie lived and worked with Helen all their waking hours.

Annie could have told the story from her point of view, but she was still busy helping Helen at Radcliffe, and John suggested there was a better way. They could publish Annie's wonderful letters to Mrs. Hopkins and make them the long conclusion to the book.

The Story of My Life was an immediate and stunning success. It was widely reviewed and translated into fifty languages. If Helen's name had not already been a household word, it would become one.

Annie was not overlooked. If the book was about Helen, it was also about Annie's genius in helping to make Helen what she had become.

Mark Twain, a personal friend of theirs, wrote to Helen:

I am charmed with your book—
enchanted. You are a wonderful
creature, the most wonderful in
the world—you and your other half
together—Miss Sullivan, I mean, for
it took the pair of you to make a
complete and perfect whole. How she
stands out in her letters! Her
brilliancy, penetration, originality,
wisdom, character—they are all there.

Annie got an equally complimentary letter from Alexander Graham Bell. "These
letters to Mrs. Hopkins," he said, "will become a standard, the principles that guided
you in the early education of Helen are of
the greatest importance to all teachers."

In the months that John Macy had spent
working with Annie and Helen on *The Story
of My Life*, he grew attached, not only to the
subject, but to Annie herself. Shortly after
the book was published, he told Annie that
he loved her and wanted to marry her.

Three and Then Two

ANNIE WAS THRILLED THAT JOHN LOVED her. She loved him, too. But she was thirty-six, ten years older than John. And then there was another problem. It was hard for her to talk about it, John could see.

"What is it?" he pressed.

Finally Annie said, "It's Helen . . ."

"If you mean that when you marry me you will have to leave her, that does not have to be. Our home could be hers. You could go on being *Teacher* for the rest of your life."

"If you will ask Helen, and if she is willing, I will say yes," Annie said.

John then went to speak with Helen.

What Helen said was that she would be very unhappy if they did *not* marry.

Annie changed her mind so many times that John almost had printed on the wedding invitation: *Subject to change without notice.*

The wedding took place on May 3, 1905. It was held in the home Annie had shared with Helen in Wrentham, Massachusetts. Twenty people attended.

The room was full of gifts and bouquets of flowers. Someone spelled the words of the service into Helen's hand. Her eyes misted over with happy tears.

Helen had by this time graduated with honors, *cum laude,* from Radcliffe College. The diploma had said that she had been particularly excellent in "English letters." Many at the graduation thought that Annie should have received a degree as well.

The three settled into their cozy farmhouse at Wrentham. Helen started to write another book and John began a book of his own. Annie and John both helped Helen with typing and editing. Annie could let her eyes rest much of the time.

They went tobogganing and horseback

riding and played many games of checkers and chess with pieces especially designed for the blind. John strung a wire from tree to tree across their property so that Helen could go for walks by herself and find her way back.

Annie had learned all the arts of southern cooking from Mrs. Keller when she lived at Tuscumbia. Friends always knew where they could get a delicious meal. And John brought many interesting people to visit. Helen's mother and Annie's beloved house-mother, Mrs. Hopkins, were also frequent guests. It was hard for Mrs. Hopkins to imagine that the sad little girl from the Tewksbury almshouse was now a hostess in what looked to her like high society! She would walk around the house, mumbling to herself in amazement, "My, oh my, oh my . . ."

The three were invited to an exposition in St. Louis, Missouri, meant to stir up interest in both deaf and blind people and to explore ways to help them.

One day was set aside as Helen Keller Day. At a meeting in her honor five hundred

were turned away because the hall could not hold them. Some imaginative people had brought stepladders and could be seen coming in through the windows.

Helen and Annie had to fight their way to the stage. People wanted to touch Helen and get close to her. By the time the two women had reached the stage, Helen's dress had been torn and some flowers plucked from her hat.

This was followed by a reception where three thousand people crammed into the vast dining room. They passed and greeted Helen and Annie. The two were dressed in contrast to each other: Annie in a black gown trimmed with jet beads, Helen in white lace. Fingers were seen flying in the air as deaf people communicated with each other through the manual language.

Many deaf people are unable to speak out loud. It is difficult for them to use their voices because they have no way of knowing if they are talking loudly or softly, high-pitched or low and rumbling. And they can't imitate sounds, because they can't hear them.

Helen had been taught to use her voice when she was still a teenager. It was a wonderful breakthrough for her. But she did not speak well and people had trouble understanding her.

Now she was determined to improve. She hired a better voice teacher and practiced with Annie for hours each day. Annie would repeat certain sounds over and over, while Helen, to feel the vibrations, placed fingers on Annie's neck, and even in the inside of her mouth!

With Helen able to speak clearly, there would be a new way for them to make a living. While some wealthy people had contributed to their finances from time to time, there was always the need to be self-supporting. And now particularly so, for they were completely alone at Wrentham.

John Macy had become restless. He spent more and more time traveling, and was almost never home. Things were going wrong in the marriage, much to Annie's sorrow.

Nine years after the happy wedding scene, John Macy left for good, and Annie and Helen were once again on their own.

Hollywood!

LECTURES WERE AT THAT TIME A VERY popular form of entertainment. There was no television. There were no movies. People crowded into lecture halls, clubhouses, theaters, to see and hear famous celebrities.

Annie and Helen became an "act." They traveled around the country and were seen by tens of thousands. The act went like this. . . .

Annie would come on stage and speak in her rich and pleasant voice, all about how she had taught Helen. Then Helen herself would appear, usually led on stage by her mother or a friend who knew the manual al-

phabet. She would rest her arm on a grand piano next to a vase filled with flowers. Then she would answer questions put to her by the audience.

Annie was in her late forties, Helen in her mid thirties. Both wore their hair pinned up and favored white dresses of a similar cut.

The very first time Helen used her voice in public, it was a nightmare for her. As she described it, "Terror invaded my flesh, my mind froze, my heart stopped beating." She made a sound that felt to her like a bomb exploding, but it was only a whisper.

With Annie's help Helen was able to regulate her voice so that everyone could understand her.

Annie and Helen traveled all over the United States and Canada. They traveled on express trains and "milk" trains, which stopped at country barns in the morning, collecting milk in cans to take to the cities.

In Texas and Louisiana, there were floods that brought water almost up to their windows. They felt a jolt every time the train hit a piece of floating lumber or a dead cow.

In the town of Bath, Maine, Annie got

very sick. A head cold had turned into the flu. Annie's last thought as she slipped into fever and delirium was *What will happen to us? What if I die? Helen can't even get home!*

When Helen could no longer feel her teacher's fingers moving against the palm of her hand, she was in a panic. It was the dead of night. She could not use a telephone. She could not find her way to the desk clerk at the hotel where they were staying. Their room was one of many in a complicated maze of hallways.

Finally, in the morning, Annie revived enough to get help. After this incident, they never went on a trip without a third person.

Wherever they went, photographers and reporters were at their heels. Once when their taxi broke down, a half dozen photographers started pulling at the door, trying to get it open.

Famous people took part in these lectures or came to meet them. Among them were Alexander Graham Bell, former President William Howard Taft, the singer Enrico Caruso, and Henry Ford.

Thomas Edison, who was largely deaf himself, asked Helen: Would she speak louder? She was able to "listen" to him by putting her fingers on his lips. He showed Annie and Helen his latest invention—the phonograph. Later Helen wrote: "He expects soon to perfect a machine that will produce 'speaking pictures'" (meaning movies).

At a fair in San Francisco, Annie was on the same platform as the Italian educator Maria Montessori. Both received "Teacher's Medals."

"I have been called a pioneer," Montessori told the crowd. Then she pointed to Annie: ". . . but there is your *real* pioneer."

A musician named George Lewis wrote a song about Helen called "Star of Happiness." It occurred to him that the two women would do well on the vaudeville circuit (vaudeville was a kind of traveling variety show very popular at the time).

They found that vaudeville was not much different from lecturing. Show times were shorter, music was added, and the pay was far higher. Annie and Helen were amused, performing on the same programs as trained seals, acrobats, and monkeys.

The bright stage lights and glitter were painful to Annie's eyes. Doctors warned her that she must stop performing or she would go totally blind. But she didn't stop until she became ill again. Her place was then taken by Polly Thomson, who had become their secretary and friend.

Then came Hollywood.

Someone had come up with the scheme of telling Helen's story on the screen. Annie and Helen were delighted. Here would be a solution to their financial problems. Doing a movie would make them rich women. They might never have to work again!

But where was the adventure in Helen's life? The romance? Audiences at that time wanted their movie scenarios written on a grand scale.

Well, if real life was not entirely satisfactory, why not add some fantasy? And so there was a scene in which a fine lady representing "Knowledge" fought a nasty fellow called "Ignorance" as they tried to win the soul of the newborn baby Helen. In another scene Helen herself played the "Mother of Sorrows," a figure something like Joan of Arc, who brings deliverance to the suffering people of the world.

Not surprisingly the title of the movie was *Deliverance*. It opened on August 18, 1919, to a packed theater on Broadway. People came in spite of a big thunderstorm.

There was just one problem. A union called Actors' Equity, which had just been formed, was out on strike. Members were picketing the theater. And so Annie and Helen did not attend their own opening because they did not want to be strikebreakers.

When a few favorable reviews came out the next morning, the women thought their troubles would be over. They would have a chauffeur-driven car, beautiful clothing, and money left over for a rainy day.

But after the first night there were no more packed houses. The movie was, in the language of the trade, a "flop."

"Quiet and Truly Great"

ANNIE AND HELEN WERE, BY THIS TIME, "hams." They knew how to hold an audience in the palms of their hands. They were like flowers ready to be plucked—for the right cause.

The cause came along in the form of the American Foundation for the Blind. Just formed in 1921, this group was a clearing-house for information about blindness and blind people, bringing together the work of several groups.

M. C. Migel, a millionaire with a heart, was the president. He knew that if he could get Helen Keller and her famous teacher to solicit funds for them, the foundation would be able to provide more help to blind people.

Migel made sure the two women were well paid—better than they had been in vaudeville, and certainly better than in Hollywood.

For the next three years they spoke at several hundred meetings, all over the country. The foundation's Helen Keller Endowment raised two million dollars.

Helen spoke about the plight of blind and deaf-blind people, who "stared into the dark with nothing but the dark staring back." Given the proper training, many of these people, now completely idle, could become skilled carpenters, builders, musicians, or select other vocations.

Annie and Helen campaigned for the Talking Book program. These were phonograph recordings of whole books, a new idea. The recordings made it easier for blind people to find information and get entertainment. Soon afterward the government produced twenty-three thousand phonographs and gave them away to blind people.

Helen kept writing books, but Annie's

eyes were now so poor that she could not help Helen very much. She was now under the care of a Dr. Berens, one of the country's leading ophthalmologists. Again, he advised her not to use her eyes. She wore thick double-lensed eyeglasses that were so heavy, she could only wear them a few hours at a time. And then there came a day when she was unable to read even with those.

Doubleday and Company came to their rescue. They supplied an editor to help with the books. Her name was Nella Braddy. Together with Annie providing help whenever she could, Nella helped Helen with her fourth book, *Midstream: My Later Life*, which told the story where *The Story of My Life* left off.

While waiting for Helen to type out drafts of the book, Nella and Annie sat and talked about Annie's own life. Why not a book about Annie? Nella suggested.

Four years later, in 1933, *Anne Sullivan Macy: The Story Behind Helen Keller* came out. (This has been the main source of information about Annie's life.)

Now in her sixties, Annie was ailing. Still

she was able to make several trips to Europe with Helen, accompanied by the faithful Polly Thomson.

Annie was able to see Ireland, the land of her parents' birth. Her heart thrilled when she finally saw the famous River Shannon, "the tear that fell from the eyes of the Lord."

As she stood at the chapel on the banks of the river, she wondered if her mother and father had been either christened or married there.

Ireland was still a land of poverty. When she saw the ships coming in and out of the harbor, she felt "heartache and tears," as she wrote:

> . . . for countless have boarded
> ships there, leaving forever the
> land of their birth. Clearly, oh
> so clearly, I heard my father bidding
> his father and mother good-bye,
> clinging to them until the ship
> pulled them apart and bounded out
> to sea.

In Yugoslavia a Helen Keller fund for blind people was started, and Annie and Helen received medals from the king. They

attended a garden party at Buckingham Palace in England, where Helen demonstrated to the British king and queen how she could "read" lips.

Back in the United States, Temple University in Philadelphia awarded Helen an honorary degree. One was offered to Annie also, but she refused it, saying that she did not have the proper education. At this ceremony Helen told the story of her study at Radcliffe College, and how Annie, after all her work there, was given no recognition. Thousands of people in the audience voted unanimously to award Annie the honorary degree.

The eyedrops the doctor had prescribed for Annie were no longer working. And Annie was getting weaker and weaker. Helen had to stay home to help take care of her. The tables were turned as Helen had to teach Annie all the letters in braille she had long since forgotten, and to read aloud to her. For "Teacher" was now completely blind!

On October 20, 1936, when Annie Sullivan was just over seventy, and the little girl she had rescued from silence and darkness was fifty-six, Annie died a peaceful death.

Services were held in a flower-filled church in New York City, with many in attendance.

"Through her remarkable work," said the minister, "her friend became a world figure. Yet all the while the teacher remained in the background, quiet and truly great."

Helen must have felt like a child all over again, as her tie to the world was torn away from her. Never again would those loving fingers spell-spell-spell into her hand. Never would they meet their friends or the hundreds and thousands of people who flocked to them, the two of them linked like sides of the same coin. It was as if the world had turned dark once again.

Yet people at the service were amazed to see Polly Thomson weeping, while Helen spelled out comforting words to *her*, with fingers flying in the air.

They wondered how Helen would manage without Annie. Helen's answer was to live a full life—one filled with drama and adventure—just as her "Teacher" would have expected.

Epilogue

THE YEAR IS 1957. ON A TELEVISION PRO-
gram called *Playhouse 90,* a made-for-TV
play is being shown. It is written by William
Gibson, a talented young playwright who
was to have several "hits" on Broadway.

The play is called *The Miracle Worker.*

The Miracle Worker is about Annie Sullivan's first weeks in Tuscumbia, Alabama,
when she and Helen fought. The battle these
two are waging is for the soul of "the wild
little animal." This battle is different than
most. In this one *both* sides will be winners.

Gibson based his play on Annie's letters in
Helen's book *The Story of My Life.* In later

times this kind of play would be called a docudrama.

The program is so successful that the play is moved to a Broadway theater, where it runs 719 performances—for almost two years!

Finally a movie is made of the play. The actresses who play the roles of Annie (Anne Bancroft) and Helen (Patty Duke) both receive Academy Awards.

Helen Keller lived for thirty-two more years after Annie died, continuing her work for blind and deaf people. She traveled in Japan, China, and Korea. After World War II, she spoke to and comforted many soldiers who had been blinded while fighting. Two more of her books were published.

And never, for a single moment, did she forget the "Teacher" and friend who had rescued her from her silent night.

"She opened the locked gates of my being," Helen wrote, "and I stretched out my hands in the quest of life."

Highlights in the Lives of
ANNIE SULLIVAN *and*
HELEN KELLER

1866 Annie is born April 14 in Feeding Hills (near Springfield), Massachusetts.

1876 Annie is sent to the Tewksbury Almshouse.

1880 Annie is admitted to the Perkins Institution for the Blind in Boston.
Helen is born June 27 in Tuscumbia, Alabama.

1881 Helen, after an illness, is left deaf and blind.

1887 Annie arrives at the Keller home in Tuscumbia, March 3.

1888 To help broaden Helen's education, Annie takes her to visit Boston and the Perkins Institution.

1900 Helen enters Radcliffe College, with Annie at her side.

1903 Helen Keller's *The Story of My Life,* edited by John Macy, is published.

1904 Helen graduates from Radcliffe.
Annie and Helen buy a farm in Wrentham, Massachusetts.

1905 Annie marries John Macy on May 3.

1919 Annie and Helen go on the vaudeville circuit.
Deliverance, a movie based on Helen's life, is produced in Hollywood.

1924 Annie and Helen begin to do work for the American Foundation for the Blind.

1929 Helen Keller's *Midstream: My Later Life,* is published.

1930 The first trips to foreign countries begin with visits to Scotland, England, and Ireland.

1933 *Anne Sullivan Macy,* Annie's life story, written by Nella Braddy, is published.

1936 Annie dies October 20.

1957 *The Miracle Worker,* a play about Annie's early work with Helen, is first produced.

1968 Helen dies June 1.

For Further Study

More Books to Read

A Girl Named Helen Keller. Margo Lundell (Scholastic)

Helen Keller. Norman Richards (Childrens Press)

Helen Keller. Richard Tames (Franklin Watts)

Helen Keller and Annie Sullivan, Working Miracles. Jon Zonderman (Blackbirch Press)

Helen Keller's Teacher. Micki Davidson (Scholastic)

The Silent Storm. Marion Marsh Brown (Abingdon Press)

Young Helen Keller: Woman of Courage. Anne Benjamin (Troll Associates)

Videos

Helen Keller. (CRM Films)

Helen Keller. (Films for the Humanities & Sciences)

Helen Keller and Her Teacher. (CRM Films)

Helen Keller In Her Story. (Phoenix/BFA Films & Videos)

Helen Keller: Voice and Vision in Her Soul. (AIMS Media)

Index

99